Scott

Battles

86 A.D. to 1746

by

George Forbes

LANG SYNE PUBLISHERS LTD.

Published by Lang Syne Publishers Ltd
Strathclyde Business Centre.
120 Carstairs Street, Glasgow G40 4DJ.
Tel: 0141 554 9944

Printed by JSB Print
107 Coltness Lane, Queenslie Industrial Estate.
Glasgow G33 4DR
Tel: 0141 766 3355

Reprinted 2001 & 2003

SCOTTISH BATTLES

CONTENTS

INTRODUCTION

Fighting and the Scots seem to have gone fist in glove since time immemorial.

They preferred fighting the English but if this was not convenient they fought rival clans or, failing that, their immediate relatives, honing the arts of war and a martial spirit over the centuries.

Whether this has something to do with the harsh climate and the need to defend one's meagre 'patch', whether it is in the racial genes, whether northern climes breed a hardier type, whether inter-action with violent incomers like the Vikings helped - all these theories can be endlessly debated.

But the fact remains that Scotland was the one country the mighty ancient Romans set out to conquer and failed dismally to do so therefore the warlike spirit of fierce independence and ferocious aggressiveness go back a long way.

And it is the country where the last battle on British soil was fought when Scottish rebels were defeated as much by their own leaders' incompetence as the professionalism of English arms.

In the following pages are gathered together a rich, exciting array of the bloodiest and most fascinating battles fought on Scottish soil over the last two thousand years.

They range widely from the inevitable clashes with Scotland's more powerful southerly neighbour to dynastic quarrels and religious disputes.

Modern readers may wonder why men were so willing to lay down their lives over arcane pieces of scripture or over fierce loyalties to distant kings with spurious claims to the throne.

As steel rings once more over the centuries and warriors in their shirt tails rampage down hillsides crimson with blood-red sunsets in their famous Highland charges, as you hear once more the war cries and the frenzied neighing of terrified horses and the clink of chain mail and the crash of grapeshot, one thing is certain and that is of the general courage, not to say recklessness, of many of the protagonists involved.

Some of the leaders may have been inspired military geniuses, some may have been arrogant idiots, but below them the ranks usually remained solid to the end and devoted to their banners over and above the call of duty.

As the United Kingdom took shape in the century following the Treaty of Union, it was left to shrewd English politicians like Pitt the

Younger to harness that splendid fighting spirit in the service of Great Britain, particularly when it came to bloody colonial wars but also most notably in winning the Peninsular War and the Battle of Waterloo.

It was, after all, the Gordons who performed a sword dance for the edification of the Duchess of Richmond at her famous ball on the eve of Napoleon's celebrated defeat (a kilted jig which must have had the old Gordons spinning in their Aberdeenshire graves) and it was the Emperor himself who declared, when he saw the Scots regiments advancing, "Who are these Amazons they are sending against me?"

The old clan traditions and esprit-de-corps was carried virtually intact into the British Army and the Scots have retained their fierce independent identity in the ranks up to the present time despite Whitehall efforts to subsume the Scots entirely in a grey, mundane mass.

But before all that, Scotland was the scene of various dramatic clashes and a selection of seventeen of them can be found in these pages.

The main battles are all here as well as some of the lesser known but equally colourful ones. Some changed history, some had little effect but all had some element of intriguing interest about them.

Now that we live in an age when battles are restricted - if they happen at all - to football grounds or demos, it gives one a new perspective to look back on an age when chivalry was a real practical thing, when men died for their religious beliefs and when freedom was a tangible force to be fought for after all else was lost.

The Scots have continued their fights, at home and abroad, in more peaceable trades and professions where blood has only been spilt metaphorically.

They continue to make their mark and it is good to look back on the days from whence that spirit came.

CHAPTER ONE

ON THE NORTH WEST FRONTIER
(Mons Graupius, 86 AD)

The first major battle recorded in Scotland took place in the first century A.D. and was a clash between the native northern tribes and the expanding Roman empire.

The Roman eagles came north, fresh from triumphs over the southern tribes but they met their match when they came up against the Picti, that strange breed of savage fighters who daubed their bodies with blue wode before charging into battle hence earning their name ('Picti' meaning 'painted people' in Latin).

Little is known about these almost mythical figures lost in the mists of time. They did leave behind a rich legacy of artistic achievement in the shape of intricately sculpted standing stones depicting allegorical monsters, interlocking serpents, battle scenes, wolves, boars, hounds, stags, horsemen, warriors and boats so they could not have been the barbaric savages depicted by their enemies. They also left jewellery and clothing yet the written records of their lifestyles are virtually non-existent or based on fabled tales.

They were descended from ancient Iron Age tribes and inhabited the lands north of the Forth and Clyde estuaries and they were also badly underestimated by the invading Romans who came across the Cheviots with 25,000 men, determined to subjugate everyone in their path and complete the conquest of Britain.

In one season's vigorous campaigning in AD 79 they swept up to the Tay and turned their faces to the vast wilderness they called Caledonia and which they said was peopled by "half-naked savages with reddish hair and large limbs".

The Roman leader on this hostile north west frontier of the Roman Empire was a general called Gnaeus Julius Agricola whose biography was written soon after his death by his son-in-law Tacitus, a celebrated historian to whom we owe most of the details concerning the military exploits in Caledonia.

The legions fought the Picts for seven years and their clash culminated in a mighty battle which was given the name Mons Graupius in AD 86.

The site of the battle has never been conclusively identified. It was close to the sea and was in the far north. A case has been made

out for its being Mount Bennachie close to Inverurie, near a large Roman marching camp at Durno located by aerial photography in the late 1970s.

Another possible site was north of Perth at the Hill of Blair.

The Picts were led by their warlord Calgacus who had a low opinion of the Romans, stating, "In them is an arrogance which no submission or good behaviour can escape. Pillagers of the world, they have exhausted the land by their plunder and now they ransack the sea. A rich enemy excites their cupidity, a poor one their lust for power. To robbery, butchery and rapine they give the lying name of 'government'; they create desolation and call it peace. We are faced by a conquering Empire that has doomed all the world to slavery. We are not yet subdued but we are the last refuge of freedom in the world. If we are conquered, it will die. And what have our enemies, in all their splendour of their arms, to match with freemen fighting for all that freemen love? On them. Let each man of you bear himself as if not only his country's fate but the liberty of the world depended on his single arm."

The Picts had around 30,000 men and the two armies faced each other across the green, grassy battlefield.

The Roman veterans were lined up in disciplined ranks, the sunlight gleaming off their iron armour.

Opposite, the restless Picts or Caledonians yelled their challenges and came streaming down the hillside, lining up their restless, undisciplined front lines on the edge of a plain with reserves on the slopes behind. On the flanks were the horsemen riding bareback on their tough, little ponies and interspersed among them were war chariots, two horses yoked in each, their wheel-hubs glinting menacingly with metal blades.

Agricola dispersed his troops in classic Roman fashion with foreign mercenaries placed to take the brunt of the enemy's charge. Eight thousand auxiliaries, highly trained, dedicated troops, formed the solid centre and three thousand cavalry were on the wings. Several elite legions were kept in reserve.

After an initial exchange of missiles, both sides advanced menacingly.

Three cohorts of Batavians and two of Tungrians moved forward, swinging their short swords, flinging themselves on the leading ranks of the Picts whose long, unwieldy weapons proved inferior in the ensuing combat at close hand.

These enthusiastic military soldiers of fortune loved their work

and were soon battling the natives back up the slope of the hill.

Calgacus then sent his chariots into action and they barged into the Roman cavalry, throwing them into confusion, crippling the terrified horses and scything down the enemy with spears and javelins. But the Pictish chariots were becoming hopelessly embroiled in the opposing ranks which gradually closed in round them.

Meanwhile, the Pictish infantry had rallied and made a counter charge, pushing the Romans back down the hill. The battle now reached a crucial stage with savage hand-to-hand fighting.

Agricola despatched his reserve cavalry who made an outflanking manoeuvre which caught out the Picts in the rear. Normally this would have resulted in a conclusive victory for the Roman tactics.

But Calgacus managed to rally his shattered ranks and they retreated in good order to the shelter of a wood where they prepared to make a last stand to the west of the plain.

They held their ground until sunset when the Romans over-ran their position and the Picts broke and took to the hills.

Technically it was a victory for the Romans but a Pyrrhic one because the invaders had been badly mauled and shocked at the strength of the resistance. They were forced to retreat south behind their line of forts and Agricola had to stay there, gazing angrily in frustration at the unconquered northlands until he was recalled to Rome a year later.

With his departure, any serious attempt to subdue the whole of Scotland evaporated. No other general among the invaders had his drive or ambition and gradually the Romans were reduced to holding the line with garrison posts, then the Antonine Wall between the Forth and Clyde, then less than forty years after Mons Graupius the Romans constructed Hadrian's Wall between the Tyne and the Solway Firth which marked the limit of their northward push.

Never at any time had the Romans kept a strong hold on Scotland. Even in the lands they had ostensibly conquered, they were kept constantly on alert fending off guerilla raids.

The Scots can certainly rightly claim that of all the countries the Romans sought to colonise their's alone successfully held out and, in the long run, defeated them.

Mons Graupius may therefore be classified as a technical set-back which led on to eventual victory.

CHAPTER TWO

BLOOD ON THE SEASHORE
(Largs, 1263)

The Vikings from Scandinavia raided Scotland for centuries during the Dark Ages and viewed the northern and western isles as their own personal fiefdom.

The kings of Scotland took it as a personal affront that these foreigners should have such a presence in a country they regarded as their own.

By the 13th century a full-scale clash of arms between the two countries seemed inevitable.

King Haco of Norway deemed it intolerable that his holdings in Argyll and the Hebrides were being placed under threat while King Alexander 111 of Scotland thought it time these intruders were kicked out.

The Scots sent ambassadors to Norway hoping the matter might be settled peacefully but Haco sent them back again with the clear message that he intended to send a powerful force to protect his territories.

He was as good as his word and in the summer of 1263 summoned the cream of the fighting men in his kingdom and more than 200 longships gathered at Bergen for the invasion.

The fleet sailed for the Orkneys where they were feasted by their countrymen. The Vikings were not put off by an eclipse of the sun which took place as they restocked their supplies and they set off for the Hebrides, wending their way slowly down the west coast, eventually anchoring in the Firth of Clyde between Arran and the Ayrshire coast.

By now autumn gales were creating havoc in the fleet while the Scots gathered their forces in the surrounding hills.

Haco, an ageing monarch, seemed to be losing control of the situation.

The weather now forced the Norsemen ashore but it was under conditions which suited the Scots.

The invaders, who should have disembarked long before at a spot suitable to their purposes, now waded ashore onto a narrow strip of rocky beach where they were confronted by their enemies on higher, more advantageous ground who rained down missiles on them.

It proved impossible for the Norsemen to deploy in any kind of organised formation while the Scots, whose army was probably nothing grander than a locally armed militia under their feudal lords stiffened by some professional men-at-arms, knew exactly what they were about, being as well organised as the invaders were disorganised.

They launched spirited frontal attacks, slaying the Vikings in bloody swathes that stained the seashore with blood. No matter how valiantly the invaders fought, there always seemed to be Scottish reinforcements pouring over the hills.

To make matters worse for the Norsemen, a gale arose and the longships were swept from their anchors, crashing into each other, while others were wrecked ashore.

In a blind panic the remnants of the Viking force fled back towards their ships, scrambling aboard as best they could and rowing away as fast as their strength would allow.

The battle had turned into a massacre although the Scottish estimate of 25,000 of the enemy slain seems to be a typical medieval exaggeration.

However, it is certainly true that no prisoners were taken.

King Haco was so shattered by this comprehensive defeat that he collapsed and died after he had reached the shelter of the Orkneys.

The Scottish King lost no time in retaking Viking lands in the west of his domain and the Earl of Mar was sent with a powerful force with orders to execute at once anyone he deemed a traitor.

Three years after the battle of Largs a formal treaty was concluded whereby Norway abandoned all claim to the Hebrides and the Viking threat that had plagued the country for so long was finally lifted.

At the same time the kingdom of Scotland was consolidated and expanded into the shape we know today.

CHAPTER THREE

A BRIDGE TOO FAR
(Stirling Bridge, 1297)

William Wallace was a towering figure in the history of Scotland's struggle for independence against England, a combination Robin Hood-style figure with the prestige of a super patriot.

He is always depicted in sculpture as brave, martial, resourceful and immensely strong and his personality was a rallying point for his beleaguered countrymen. His own misadventures coincided with the political setbacks of his country and his life saw a fusion of both into a trail of glory and bloodshed which had many high points but ended in tragedy.

Scotland's troubles began in earnest when in the year 1286 the horse of King Alexander 111 stumbled at Kinghorn, flinging the rider off and killing him.

His untimely demise, with both his sons dead before him, left as his only heir his grand-daughter, the eight-year-old Princess Margaret of Norway.

Needless to say, this fatal accident now plunged the country into chaos.

Six 'Guardians of the Kingdom' were appointed to supervise a regency council and arrange for Margaret to be brought to her new realm.

But a Scottish baron, Robert the Bruce, Lord of Annandale, who was a descendant on his mother's side from King David l, claimed it was not lawful for a female to wear the crown and claimed the throne as his own.

Various nobles joined him, he raised a motley army and several garrisons in the south of Scotland were seized.

The country was torn by civil war.

The Guardians made the mistake of appealing to King Edward 1st of England for help. He was a cruel, vain, ambitious, ruthless man and he was quick to suggest that Margaret marry his son, the Prince of Wales, thereby solving the problems by producing a ready-made King of Scotland.

This scheme which would have brought Scotland under the yoke of her more powerful southern neighbour might have succeeded if Margaret had not died on her trip over from Norway.

The throne was now vacant once more and no less than thirteen claimants to it arose, squabbling incessantly amongst themselves.

The only solution to the problem seemed to be to appoint an arbiter and, of course, Edward put himself forward.

His role was accepted by the claimants, all of them keen to utilise his support and get in his favour.

Edward eventually chose John Balliol who had a better claim than his nearest rival, Bruce.

The judgement was accepted, Balliol duly did homage to Edward and was crowned King of Scotland.

The English now planned a military campaign in France and Edward called on the Scots for support but Balliol, under pressure from his subjects, reneged on his alliance with the English and declared that he would be entering into an alliance with the French.

Naturally, the English were furious and an invasion force was quickly despatched north. They easily outnumbered the disorganised Scots and defeated them at Dunbar.

Edward now garrisoned the countryside and viewed Scotland as an extension of his kingdom, insult being added to injury by the appointment of the Earl of Surrey as Scottish Guardian with other Englishmen in top positions.

The Scottish nobles owned large tracts of land south of the border and were loathe to loose these by any show of disloyalty so there was no lead given to the common folk by the aristocracy when it came to the country gaining independence.

That kind of rebellious spirit could only be found among the lesser nobles, among which was the young, fiery William Wallace.

He was the second son of a modest knight from Elderslie near Paisley but his family had never been very rich or powerful so in one sense Wallace had little to lose.

Energetic, immune to fatigue, quick tempered and ferocious, from an early age Wallace had fostered a deep, bitter hatred against the English.

When he looked at his country suffering under their rule, he took a decision at the age of 24 to take to the hills with a band of outlaws and begin a guerilla war against the occupying forces.

In May, 1297, he murdered the Sheriff of Lanark, allegedly over the death of his sweetheart, and he was declared a renegade.

His forces grew in numbers and English fortresses were attacked, supply wagons robbed and patrols ambushed.

Wallace's example proved a rallying point for Scottish resistance and the English forces increasingly began to take him seriously.

Edward determined to stamp out this rebel army as quickly as possible and sent a powerful force north to teach them a strict lesson.

The behaviour of the English troops was so violent against the native population that popular resistance to their incursion grew and the numbers of Wallace's supporters increased daily.

From a vagrant band of bowmen in Selkirk Forest, the rebel now had an organised army which took a series of castles in quick succession from Glasgow to Montrose. They were busy laying siege to Dundee when they heard that the English host were approaching Stirling and Wallace at once resolved to take on the invaders.

The bridge at Stirling was a wooden construction which was so narrow that only two horsemen could pass over it at one time and the Scots had sabotaged the supports at the north end so that a few hammer blows would suffice to bring the whole construction crashing into the river below.

As the English arrived, they noted the Scottish forces were ranged over Abbey Craig where the Wallace Monument now stands.

Wallace's forces amounted to forty thousand infantry and a hundred and eighty knights. The English had fifty thousand foot soldiers and a thousand knights.

The armies settled down for the night. The English commanders were Surrey and Cressingham, one lethargic, the other arrogant and brash, both convinced their army's reputation and superior numbers would be enough to over-awe the Scots.

They sent over priests to demand surrender but Wallace sent them back with the message, "Tell your people we have not come here to gain peace but for battle to avenge and deliver our country. Let them come up when they like and they will find us ready to meet them beard to beard."

At dawn five thousand English foot soldiers crossed the bridge but Surrey was still calmly asleep in his tent so rather than be caught out exposed on the wrong bank of the river they quickly made their way back over to the south side again.

When Surrey eventually stirred himself an hour later he was given conflicting counsel. An old soldier, Sir Richard Lundin, who had deserted from the Scottish ranks, pointed out to him the hazards of a slow crossing of the bridge with a prepared enemy on the other side and offered to show him a ford downriver where a large force could pass over quickly. But Cressingham, who was the Treasurer as well as an arrogant priest, pressed for immediate action even although he had no military experience, claiming that delay was wasting the King's money. Surrey, in his indolent way, listened to the more powerful priest and gave the order to cross over the bridge at once, with Cressingham leading the way.

Slowly, the cumbersome English army made its way over the wooden structure.

Wallace, watching closely from the heights opposite, held his hand and the English knights, mistakenly viewing this inaction as cowardice, decided to charge the Scots even although only half of the English army had crossed over.

Meanwhile, Wallace had secretly sent a small band of men down to the end of the bridge where the supports had been weakened. They quickly smashed through the wood, sending the bridge plunging into the river, drowning many enemy troops.

The English forces were now cut in two and crucially they were outnumbered on the north side of the river where the Scots forces charged down on them.

The English knights and infantry had been exhausted by their charge across difficult terrain and their ranks broke with the Scots, yelling and screaming, their claymores and battle axes swirling, smashing into them, cutting and slashing with their ferocious weapons, soaking the green grass with red English blood.

Cressingham was one of the first to fall and his body was later skinned, pieces being torn off as trophies of vengeance.

No prisoners were taken as the trapped English forces were hacked to pieces, few of them managing to fight their way back to the southern side of the river.

Surrey could only watch on helplessly as the swords glittered in the distance and the clamour of battle wafted in his direction.

A sudden panic now seized his forces as they witnessed the carnage and wholesale slaughter taking place opposite. They broke and fled, leaving their baggage trains to the enemy, and they did not stop retreating until they had reached the safety of Berwick Castle which was the nearest English stronghold.

Surrey had lost twenty thousand men to the weapons of the Scots. Their bodies were piled up at the foot of Abbey Craig.

It had been a comprehensive victory which put Wallace in supreme control of Scotland.

It also illustrated how, with a bit of guile, the Scots could be victorious against the larger numbers of their enemies and how disciplined infantry properly positioned could decimate knights.

These were all lessons that the Scots took to heart in the years ahead.

CHAPTER FOUR

THE STEEL CIRCLES
(Falkirk, 1298)

The victory at Stirling Bridge brought new hope to Scottish patriots and raised their morale.

This was increased with the surrender of important castles at Dundee, Roxburgh and Edinburgh and within a few weeks the English had been cleared out of all the strongholds in Scotland.

Wallace became regent but he refused to act alone and took the young Sir Andrew Moray as his colleague.

Neighbourhoods raised levies of troops to defend the realm, the recruits being aged from 16 to 60 and gibbets were erected to encourage any ditherers, a ploy which proved so successful that a standing army was quickly assembled.

Wallace was so confident of its military prowess that he ordered an invasion of England and the Scottish forces swarmed into Berwick and Northumbria, laying waste the land. He laid siege to Carlisle but the garrison held out and, with Winter coming on, the Scottish army contented itself with ravaging Cumberland and Durham before carrying off their spoils back up north over the border.

This ravaging had lasted a couple of months during which time the English had mustered a force of twenty thousand under Lord Robert Clifford who tracked after the Scottish army.

The English forces crossed over into Annandale and laid it waste as revenge for the Scots actions then returned back south.

Meanwhile, King Edward, busy with the English army in Flanders, heard the news of Wallace's depredations and hastened home in a savage mood, summoning a parliament to meet at London to discuss the situation.

Edward put his problems in France in abeyance and handed over the problem to the Pope to sort out, being eager to teach the recalcitrant Scots a lesson once and for all that they would not forget.

In June, 1298, Edward's army assembled at Newcastle and a month later they crossed the Tweed at Berwick and made their way slowly northwards, establishing a camp at Kirkliston.

When he heard that the Scots were gathering at Falkirk, Edward, ever aggressive when it came to waging war, advanced to Linlithgow.

THE STEEL CIRCLES

On the eve of battle Edward, who had been lying sleeping on the ground, was trampled by his horse, picketed beside him, sustaining two broken ribs. But this did not prevent him leading his troops into battle. He well deserved his title 'Hammer of the Scots'.

Wallace had troops garrisoned throughout the countryside and when his army was assembled it was discovered that their numbers were half that of the English. He should have retreated but this might have proved even costlier in casualties than standing still, such was the speed of the English onslaught powered by Edward's anger.

Wallace hastily organised his men into the old Scottish formation of 'schiltrons' which involved the troops being formed into large circles with ranks of tight-knit spears and lances projecting outwards. This was an extremely difficult obstacle for either cavalry or infantry to penetrate or sweep aside.

Between four of these schiltrons Wallace positioned the Selkirk bowmen and on the flanks were the cavalry, a small force under Sir John Comyn.

A little stream separated the two armies and a bog lay in front of the Scottish army which for a short time deterred Edward in his planning. But his knights were keen to get to grips with the enemy while the English were numerically superior so Edward jumped astride his charger, yelling, "On, then, in God's name - and may the day be ours!"

An English column then flung itself at the Scottish centre but became literally bogged down in marshland as Edward had feared. Other troops made more successful flanking attacks and Comyn was forced to flee or fight and be massacred.

Three more English divisions charged the Scottish line while arrows showered down on them.

Meantime, English long-bows took a heavy toll of the Scottish troops jammed in the schiltrons and slingers using rocks also cut holes in Wallace's ranks.

Men-at-arms fought and chopped their way through the enemy ranks and by sheer weight of numbers the battle swung their way.

With the Scottish cavalry dissipated and the archers being gradually whittled down to a pile of bodies, only the steel circles remained but gradually holes appeared in these, gaps just large enough for Edward's cavalry to go pouring through. Once this happened, the schiltrons were split asunder and the Scots were cut down in crimson swathes.

The end of the battle came very quickly with the breaking of these steel rings.

Wallace with a small bodyguard managed to gallop to safety across the bloodstained grass to the shelter of a nearby wood and from there he retreated to Stirling, setting it ablaze before retiring into the hills.

But it was a Pyrrhic victory for Edward who rampaged around, laying waste Fife and the Borders before returning home.

Falkirk proved the end for Wallace. His prestige had been shattered and other leaders arose to lead his people. He wasted his time on a fruitless trip to the Continent to seek help from the Pope and the French King but to no avail although the former wrote to Edward castigating him for his belligerency against Scotland which was a free sovereign nation.

When he returned home Wallace was betrayed and seized by English troops.

A show trial at Westminster ended with Wallace being hung, drawn and quartered and parts of his body being displayed throughout the land. It was a grotesque end for a brave fighting man and indicative of the fear in which he was held by his enemies.

CHAPTER FIVE

THE GREAT VICTORY
(Bannockburn, 1314)

With Wallace's death, the Norman knight and claimant to the Scottish throne, Robert the Bruce, stepped out of the shadows and took centre stage as the focal point of his countrymens' aspirations.

He had very real grounds on which to claim kingship, his grandfather having been chosen by the childless King Alexander 11 as a successor to the royal line (the Bruces being descended from King David 1st).

Other claimants had superseded the Bruces over the years but with the struggles over the Scottish throne reaching a climax towards the end of the 13th century Robert the Bruce believed his time had come.

He was fierce, proud, charismatic, a born leader of men, impatient and, above all, ambitious.

Obviously there was much to lose by defying the English but Bruce considered the gamble well worth taking.

Initially, he played a canny game between Edward and Wallace, swapping sides depending on the tides of fortune as it affected both warriors. This was routine behaviour on the parts of knights at this time whose loyalty was as variable as their moods.

But the end that Bruce always had in view was the Scottish throne and he behaved in a way which he felt would advance this ambition.

Involved in secret planning and plotting to advance the Scottish cause, Bruce was finally forced to come out in the open when he stabbed to death another claimant to the throne, the Red Comyn, after a ferocious quarrel in Greyfriars' Church, Dumfries.

Bruce was now an outlaw on the run. The Comyns were a force to be reckoned with and they were out for vengeance.

With a handful of loyal followers, Bruce sought sanctuary from Bishop Wishart in Glasgow who was a prelate with a strong military streak in him, having taken the field against the English and broken several oaths of loyalty to them.

Not only did Wishart obligingly give absolution for the murder of Comyn but he urged Bruce to have himself crowned King of Scots at Scone.

So it was that on 29th March, 1306, the golden crown was laid on

Bruce's head.

But the first few months of his reign did not augur well for the future.

His meagre army, more a body of troops, was ambushed at Methven near Perth by an English force and Bruce narrowly escaped with his life, taking to the Highland hills as a fugitive. His brother Nigel and 16 of his leading knights were all summarily hanged as traitors. Bruce's wife, daughter and sisters were taken prisoner.

With a price on his head and hunted from glen to glen, Bruce led a furtive, desperate existence for almost a year, his physical stamina and powerful, inspiring, ever optimistic personality standing him in good stead during these bleak months. He read French tales of chivalry and derring-do to keep up the spirits of his depressed followers and gradually built up a following until, with a thousand men behind him, he felt strong enough to face the English once more, defeating them in a battle at Loudon Hill.

Gradually, the Scottish nobles realised they had a true king among men in their midst and they rallied to his banner, bringing with them badly needed fighting men.

One by one the English garrisons were over-run until by 1314 the only remaining strongholds were the castles at Stirling, Berwick and Bothwell.

The old 'Hammer of the Scots' had died of dysentery which was fortunate for Bruce. The new King of England, Edward 11, had none of his father's talent for war and was also at loggerheads with his own barons over his favourite, Piers Gaveston, who was eventually executed.

Stirling Castle was held by Sir Philip Mowbray and was besieged for months by Edward Bruce, Robert's brother, until it was on the point of surrender.

On 11th June the English forces assembled on the Tweed determined to relieve Mowbray's garrison.

Around 50,000 of the best fighting men England could muster, including the flower of their chivalric nobility, rode north with all the panoply and stately show they could display.

They easily occupied Edinburgh by 21st June and the following night they were in Falkirk. The need to relieve Stirling Castle gave urgency to their normally slow progress.

Bruce's scouts kept a wary eye on the progress of the English and the Scots duly took up position at the Bannock burn, blocking Edward's march on Stirling.

Between the two armies lay bogland which was bound to hamper the heavily laden English knights.

The Scottish force was only a third that of the English and needed every ploy to gain a victory.

They therefore dug pits concealed with sods in which were hidden sharp wooden stakes and these were to create havoc among the horses of Edward's cavalry.

The Scots only had five hundred mounted knights on their right commanded by Sir Robert Keith.

The English army arrived on the scene on the afternoon of Sunday 23rd June, exhausted after their march and sweltering in the summer sunshine. They decided to postpone their attack for 24 hours.

But in the meantime a squadron of heavy English cavalry, three hundred strong, tried to outflank the Scots and get to the castle. However, five hundred pikemen stood in their way. There was a ferocious clash in which the Scots valiantly stood their ground, unhorsing the heavily armoured knights, who came crashing to the ground to be skewered with swiftly moving daggers, before the Black Douglas came galloping to help out with his men. The English retreated, badly mauled and demoralised, and first blood had gone to the Scots, considerably raising their morale.

On another part of the field there now occurred one of the most famous incidents in all Scottish history.

The Earl of Gloucester with the English advance guard had pressed forward from the main body of the army and his young knights, some of whom had been newly honoured at the beginning of this campaign as was the common feudal custom, were literally straining at the leash.

Bruce, mistakenly thinking an all-out attack was imminent, was riding up and down the front of his line on a light palfrey, steadying and encouraging his men. Sir Henry de Bohun, one of these knights, spotted the gold glinting on Bruce's helmet and realised who was before him. Without waiting for any order, de Bohun, seeking personal glory through killing the Scottish leader, spurred on his horse, his lance lowered and charged forward towards Bruce. The latter, realising at once his predicament, calmly stood his ground, waited until the English knight was thundering down on him then skillfully pulled his horse aside. De Bohun was carried on helplessly by the weight of his momentum and, as he passed, Bruce raised himself in his stirrups and brought his battle-axe crashing down onto the Englishman's skull with such force that his helmet was cleft in two and the blade sliced down to the knight's neck. As de Bohun's corpse fell off in a fountain of blood, an audible groan arose from the ranks of the English while the Scots cheered lustily. Bruce had fearlessly achieved a tremendous psychological boost for his troops and had at the same time sickened the English.

The first light of day revealed activity among both armies. The Scots knelt for mass and Edward thought they were asking for mercy but one old knight, Ingelram de Umfraville, put him right, "They do - but not of you. These men will win all or die."

The English crossed the Bannock and drew up in nine divisions, the foremost commanded by the Earl of Gloucester.

The Scots formed into three lines of spearmen called 'schiltrons' commanded by Edward Bruce, Randolph and Douglas. Bruce was with the reserve Highlanders and Islemen and the native levies of his own beloved Carrick.

The battle began with a series of reckless, brave charges led by Gloucester's cavalry against divisions commanded by Edward Bruce. The horsemen broke on a solid wall of Scottish spearmen who held their ground and fought back ferociously. Gloucester himself was killed as were many of his best knights while another English division swept down on Randolph's men only to be stopped and forced back in the same manner. Douglas moved forward in support and the massed ranks were locked in brutal, ferocious, merciless, hand-to-hand fighting.

English archers and slingers came forward and decimated the ranks of Edward Bruce before being comprehensively swept from the field by a wild charge of Keith's horsemen.

King Edward had shown himself a poor tactician. His front was far too narrow and he was unable to deploy his superior numbers properly or outflank the Scots.

His position became more precarious as harassed troops fell back, crushing and jamming those behind who were unable to use their weapons properly.

Scottish pikes cut bloody swathes in the English ranks while the hidden pits did their limb crushing work and screaming horses were swallowed up by the ground while their riders were trampled underfoot.

Scottish archers poured showers of arrows into the crushed English ranks, sitting targets for the expert bowmen.

That indefinable feeling of elation which can come over a winning army now swept the Scottish troops as they quickly realised the day could be theirs' while the English became more and more demoralised.

Bruce now committed all his reserves to swing the battle his way once and for all and at the same time his camp followers - squires, cooks, labourers - came charging over the hill, fired by the prospect of loot as much as patriotism, and the hard-pressed English troops saw through the dust and confusion of battle what they took to be reinforcements. This was the last straw and they turned and fled.

There have been recent theories that it was a troop of Knights Templar coming to re-inforce Bruce that turned the battle, the argument being that the proud English would not flee at the approach of mere camp followers. This is based on the fact that Bruce undoubtedly gave sanctuary to the Templars when they were persecuted in other countries and they settled in many parts of Scotland. It has even been argued that Bruce's technique in defeating de Bohun was an old Templar trick learned by them during the Crusades in Palestine. It is feasible that the Templars could have arrived late on the scene and played a crucial role but until there is conclusive evidence (highly unlikely since it has not arisen up till now) it will have to remain simply an intriguing theory.

Whatever the cause, the English retreated in disarray and the rout turned into a massacre as men were trampled underfoot in the rush to escape while others were slaughtered by the triumphant Scots.

Edward just managed to escape.

His attendant, Sir Giles de Argentine, told him that the battle was lost and that he must save himself, adding, "For myself, I am not used to flee nor will I do so now. I commend you to God." He spurred his horse into the thick of the fighting and was duly killed.

Surrounded by a bodyguard of loyal knights, Edward then cut a way through some Scottish infantry, which was dispersed and more interested in pursuing the main bulk of the army, and galloped off to Dunbar where he did not consider himself safe until he was on board a ship bound for Berwick.

Few Englishmen escaped the slaughter that bloody day. Among the corpses piled high on the field were 21 barons and 700 knights. There were some prisoners taken - those who could purchase their own freedom - and these included 22 barons and 60 knights.

It was a decisive victory, the most glorious in Scottish history and is still celebrated by patriots. It led within a few years to the recognition of Scottish independence and the deeds performed that day resound still in the nation's psyche.

CHAPTER SIX

ILL MET BY MOONLIGHT
(Otterburn, 1388)

The border countryside between Scotland and England was the setting for ferocious fighting over the centuries, much of that lawless area being labelled 'debatable lands' claimed by both nations and constantly changing hands throughout medieval times.

The Borders bred wild, bloodthirsty types of outlaws known as reivers whose main pastime was cattle rustling and various clans like the Armstrongs and the Douglases became notorious for their raiding parties south into England where the leading 'riding family' were the Percies.

Frequently these raids were bolstered by much larger forces as the two nations clashed.

In the mid-1380s the French, finding themselves hard pressed by the English in their own country, resolved to send an army into Scotland to assist that nation in making war upon their southern neighbours, thus diverting the latter back to their home borders.

The French sent one thousand men-at-arms and twelve hundred suits of armour with a large sum of money to assist the Scots to make war. This great force was commanded by John De Vienne, High-Admiral of France, a brave and distinguished general.

In the meantime, the King of England, Richard 11, who was bitter, ruthless and inhuman in his attitude to his enemies, summoned together a larger army than any King of England had ever before commanded and moved towards the Scottish Border country.

The Scots also assembled large forces and the French general expected there would be a great battle. He said to the Scottish nobles, "You have always said that if you had some hundreds of French men-at-arms to help you, you would give battle to the English. Now here we are to give you aid - let us give battle!"

The Scottish nobles answered that they would not risk the fate of the country in one battle. One of them, William, the Earl of Douglas, conveyed John de Vienne to a narrow pass where, unseen themselves, they might spy on the army of England marching through. The Scot pointed out the great multitude of archers, the number and high discipline of the English men-at-arms and then asked the Frenchman, as soldier, whether he could advise the Scots to oppose these archers with a few ill-trained Highland bowmen or place their small, trotting nags against the onset of the brilliant chivalry of England.

The Admiral de Vienne admitted the risk was too unequal. "But yet, if you do not fight," he said, "what do you mean to do? If you do not oppose this great force, the English will destroy your country."

"Let them do their worst," said Douglas, smiling. "They will find but little to destroy. Our people are all retired into woods, hills and morasses and have driven off their cattle - which is their only property - along with them. The English will find nothing either to take away or to eat. The houses of the gentlemen are small towers with thick walls which even fire will not destroy; as for the common people, they dwell in mere huts and if the English choose to burn them a few trees from the wood is all that is necessary to build them up again."

"But what will you do with your army if you do not fight?" said the Frenchman, "and how will your people endure the distress, famine and plunder which must be the consequences of the invasion?"

"You should see that our army will not lie idle," replied Douglas, "and as for our Scottish people they will endure pillage, famine and every extremity of war - but they will never endure an English master!"

The great army of England entered Scotland on the eastern side of the frontier and marched on, much distressed for want of provisions, laying waste the villages and what property they could but finding very little to destroy and nothing to subsist upon.

No sooner did the Scottish nobles learn the English were engaged in Scotland than with an army consisting chiefly of light cavalry they burst into the western counties of England where they did more damage in the course of a day or two's march than the English could have done in Scotland had they burned the whole country from the Borders to Aberdeen.

It was from prudence not from want of courage that the Scots avoided pitched battles with the superior forces of the English. They readily engaged in smaller actions when they fought with the utmost valour till sword and lance could endure no longer.

But in 1388 a desperate battle proved unavoidable.

After Richard 11 had personally led an army into Scotland, burning down the abbeys of Melrose, Dryburgh and Newbattle and "ravaging all things in his pride, sparing nothing, saving nothing and having no mercy on age or on religion" the Scottish nobility vowed vengeance and held a Great War Council in Edinburgh. The prospect of a booty-laden jaunt into Northumbria also whetted their appetites.

At Yetholm near Jedburgh there assembled around forty thousand warriors including a thousand cavalry, the pride of Scottish chivalry.

The army split into two. The main body under the Earl of Fife marched down through Liddesdale and towards Carlisle. A smaller group, five thousand strong and commanded by Douglas, were to make a diversionary attack on Newcastle.

Pushing through Northumbria, Douglas scarcely halted until he had reached Durham, burning and pillaging as he went, his path clearly marked by the thick rising smoke issuing from raided villages.

Percy, Earl of Northumberland and arch enemy of the Douglases, sent his two sons Sir Henry and Sir Ralph to stop the progress of this invasion. Both were gallant knights but the first, who from his impetuosity was called Hotspur, was one of the most distinguished fighters in England.

The brothers arrived behind the thick walls of Newcastle, determined to defend that vital town. They viewed the Douglas incursion as the vanguard of the main Scottish army and were determined to hold this important stronghold.

They were unaware of the fact that Douglas had no siege machinery with him and no means of conquering such an awesome obstacle.

But when Douglas arrived below the high walls of Newcastle, neither he nor Harry Percy were content merely to glower at each other across a moat sixty feet broad.

Percy sent out a challenge to Douglas offering to meet him in single combat.

A jousting list was hastily erected and under the view of both massed armies the pair clashed, mounted on their armoured warhorses.

They crashed together and Douglas unhorsed Percy. He did not kill him, however, as the code of chivalry would have allowed him to do. Instead, he grasped the pennant from his opponent's spear and fixed it on his own lance. He shook it aloft and declared that he would carry it back into Scotland and plant it on his castle at Dalkeith.

"That," yelled Percy, still prone on the ground, "shalt thou never do. I will regain my lance ere thou canst get back to Scotland!"

"Then," said Douglas, "come to seek it and thou shalt find it before my tent."

Realising their stay before Newcastle would prove fruitless, Douglas led his army on a retreat back up the Vale of the River Reed which afforded a tolerable road running northwestward toward their own frontier.

They encamped at Otterburn, twenty miles from the Scottish border, on the 19th August, 1388.

Percy, who quickly realised what was afoot, mustered a force of 600 cavalry and 8,000 infantry and set off in hasty pursuit, desperate to wreak vengeance on Douglas.

The Scottish camp was on a hillock with marshland in front of it and was fortified in a makeshift fashion. Percy's pennant fluttered outside Douglas's tent as the Scot had said it would.

A full moon arose and such was Percy's dash and impatience that, when his forces arrived within sight of the Scottish camp, he decided to begin the action right away without waiting for daylight.

The alarm was raised among the Scots who saw their enemies advancing towards their left flank.

Showing commendable discipline and resolute calmness in the feverish darkness, Douglas drew his troops up in proper battle order to face the enemy who were coming upon them as fast as possible.

The night air was rent with battle cries of "A Percy! A Percy!" only to be answered with the resounding "A Douglas! A Douglas!"

The superior forces of the English swept onto the Scottish ranks and gradually forced them back.

But Douglas himself turned the tide by charging forward, clearing his way with the blows of his battle-axe and breaking into the very thickest of the enemy.

His example inspired his men and they followed him, ferociously hacking their way into the startled English ranks who had thought victory was within their grasp.

But Douglas had been struck three mortal blows - three spear wounds in his chest and, because he had rushed into battle without taking the time to don his helmet, a savage wound received from an iron mace disfigured his head.

In the confusion the English were unaware that Douglas had fallen and the Scots carried him to the rear.

A priest called William of Berwick, the chaplain of Douglas, was protecting the body of his wounded patron with a long lance when a Scottish knight galloped up and said to the expiring leader, "How fares it, cousin?"

"Indifferently," answered Douglas. "But blessed be God, my ancestors have died in fields of battle not on down beds. I sink fast but let them still shout my war-cry - and conceal my death from my followers. There was a tradition in our family that a dead Douglas should win a field. I trust it will be this day accomplished!"

He died and his men quietly laid the body in a bracken bush so that the clashing armies would be unaware of what had happened.

The nobles returned to the fray, yelling their war-cries louder than before.

The armies battled on until sunrise when the Percy brothers were disarmed and taken prisoner and the English forces became demoralised.

The Scots now swept triumphant over the scene and almost no man of note amongst the English forces escaped death or captivity.

A Scottish poet has said of the name of Douglas glorified on this day:-

'Hosts have been known at that dread sound to yield,
And Douglas dead, his name hath won the field.'

The chronicler Froissart, who heard eye-witness accounts of the fray said that "of all the battles which I have made mention of in this history, this of Otterburn was the bravest and the best contested; for there was neither knight nor squire but acquitted himself nobly, doing well his duty, and fighting hand to hand without either stay or faintheartedness."

It was estimated more than 1,800 Englishmen were slain and among the vast numbers of prisoners were many of the wealthiest knights of the northern counties. Their ransoms proved extremely lucrative for some of the Border clans.

The body of Douglas was carried home mournfully by his followers and buried in Melrose Abbey among his forebears but he was the noblest bearer of his family name.

CHAPTER SEVEN

THE FLOWERS OF THE FOREST
(Flodden, 1513)

King James the Fourth of Scotland was never an admirer of his brother-in-law Henry the Eighth of England and observers forecast that their two countries would soon be at war.

Henry had not donated a portion of his sister's dowry but there were deeper clashes of personality between the pair which made the peace that existed between their kingdoms even more tenuous than usual.

Then in the summer of 1513 Henry, headstrong and ambitious, invaded France whose Queen appealed to James's well-known sense of chivalry to come to her rescue by invading England.

The Scottish forces duly mustered in Edinburgh but already there were strange portents.

A man in a blue gown appeared to James in St. Michael's Church in Linlithgow warning about the outcome of a war with England.

And a mysterious voice was heard one midnight in the Mercat Cross in Edinburgh as the great guns were being shipped out of the capital, commanding "earle, lord, barone and gentillman" to appear before the Devil within 40 days.

Older, wiser heads amongst James's entourage also warned against foolhardy actions but they were over-ruled by those thrilled at the prospect of striking a blow against 'the auld enemy' and garnering spoils from the English army.

Towards the end of August the Scottish army crossed the Tweed and after a six day assault Norham Castle fell to them, quickly followed by the keeps at Wark, Etal and Ford. It seemed as though the Scots were unstoppable.

Henry, who had entrusted the Earl of Surrey with keeping the Borders quiescent, also gave him charge of the English army which was to stop the Scots.

Surrey had problems marching northwards due to rainy weather which turned the trackless wastes into quagmires and bogged down his wagons and horses.

Messages were now exchanged between the two armies and it was agreed that battle would be joined on Friday, September 9th.

The Scots gathered on Flodden Hill overlooking the River Till and

Surrey set up camp six miles away.

Each side had around 25,000 men but the Scots had the advantage of being firmly established on a natural fortress which they had reinforced with a ditch and a parapet, their guns pointing downhill. On their left was the river and on the right a stretch of bogland.

Surrey, realising that the position might have to be taken by a bloody charge uphill, tried appealing to James's romantic sense of chivalry and suggested both armies meet on even ground below the hill where the odds would be more fairly distributed. For the last time during this campaign, James used common sense and told Surrey he would "take and keep his ground and field at his own pleasure".

Surrey now decided that his best hope would involve a wide flanking movement round the Scottish position which would result - if successful - in his troops catching the enemy in their unguarded rear.

The English artillery was inferior to the Scots who had seventeen heavy guns, seven of them so unwieldy that they needed 36 oxen each to drag them along. But they were the last word in gunnery at that time.

Both sides were armed with pikes but the English had more expert bowmen and also their infantry were adept in the use of the halberd or spear-axe which could cleave armour and smash metal.

The ensuing battle was to be fought entirely on foot in weather which changed capriciously from sunshine to torrential rain and the warriors often struggled in their bare feet or stockings after casting off slippery shoes in the mud.

In the early hours of September 9th Surrey began deploying his troops in their outflanking movement but he was quickly spotted by Scottish scouts who brought the news to James.

Incredibly, he did nothing about it despite the pleas of his artillery experts that they wanted to blast the English ranks strung out and exposed as they forded the river. The Scots from their vantage point now had victory in their grasp if they moved quickly but the appeal to James's chivalric nature earlier that week seems to have stuck some silly, sentimental chord with him and he refused to move against Surrey when his opponent was so obviously at a disadvantage. Well has it been said that James was a relic from a past, more idealistic age.

Meanwhile, Surrey could scarcely believe his luck that his manoevres were going ahead unopposed.

The nobility continued to appeal to James to forget his better nature but all the Earl of Angus was gruffly told by the King was, "If you are afraid, you may go home."

Others were told if they did not shut up they would be charged with treason.

As the day waned James eventually decided to do something and ordered his men to move towards a nearby hill to block the English action.

The Scots assembled in five divisions with the King in the middle. On the left were the Border divisions of Home and Huntly, on the right were the Highlanders under Lennox and Argyll. Behind the centre was a reserve commanded by Bothwell.

The English lines, a quarter of a mile away downhill, were in two rows with the centre rear commanded by Surrey.

The battle commenced in late afternoon after a brief artillery duel. It was found the Scottish guns could not be depressed enough to make any serious damage while the English round-shot was devastating.

Rather than see his lines shot to pieces, James ordered a general advance of the line and the Scots rushed furiously onto the English who were flung back by the shock of the charge.

There was now desperate hand-to-hand fighting with spears, pikes and halberds slashing at packed ranks.

James took upon himself the role of dashing hero and made a reckless charge towards the English centre where Surrey stood with his son.

Flanked by a bodyguard of nobles, James tried to hack his way to the main English standard. The power of the Scots charge meant that the Scottish King came within grasping distance of Surrey.

At this point, with both sides being staunchly bolstered with reinforcements, the battle could have gone either way.

But the Highlanders began to wither under a fussilade of English arrows and they rushed madly forward, waving their claymores and yelling their war-cries. When they hit the English ranks they created havoc but a flanking move brought up reinforcements which crashed into their sides and scattered them.

Gradually, the English forces had managed to encircle James and the remnants of his forces and kept them in a ring of steel which now closed in.

James continued fighting in the forefront, wielding a spear until it broke in his hands then drawing a sword and trying to get to Surrey's banner once more.

But at last he collapsed, several arrows protruding from his body, his left hand hanging loose from his arm, his neck gashed open, only a spear's length from Surrey.

The English now closed in for the kill but the Scots line remained unbroken even although it shrank inwards. Every Scot who fell tried to take as many English with him as possible.

Darkness crept down as the Scottish bodies piled up round the dead King and his trampled banner.

Eventually, Surrey withdrew a little distance from the slaughter, prepared to resume the massacre the following day.

But the sun only rose on the dead.

A group of a thousand Scots rallied near the Tweed but were allowed to retreat northwards as the English were too exhausted to do anything about them.

More than ten thousand Scots had been slain and it was a defeat which sent shockwaves throughout the country.

It was not simply the quantity but also the quality of those who had died which was so shocking to the Scottish nation - one King, two bishops, two abbots, twelve earls, thirteen lords, the five eldest sons of peers and the leaders of most of the country's top families.

The English took the King's corpse south where it lay within a lead coffin for many years until an Elizabethan glazier cut off the head and used it as a potpourri.

The famous poem 'The Flowers Of The Forest', commemorating the debacle, is a lament for all those who fell at Flodden. For many years it was thought to be an authentic 16th century ballad though some had their doubts. Eventually it was discovered that it had been written in the mid-18th century by Jane Elliot Minto in Teviotdale.

Its final verse goes:-

'The flowers of the forest that fought aye the foremost,
The prime o' our land now lie cauld in the clay.
We'll hear nae mair liltin' at our yowe-milkin',
Women and bairns are dowie and wae;
Sighin' and moanin' on ilka green loanin',
The flowers of the forest are a' wede away.'

It was made into a haunting pipe tune.

The flower of Scottish manhood perished on that rainy, windswept hillside in the Borders. Bannockburn, in the eyes of the English, had been amply avenged.

From the Scottish point of view the only positive aspect of the battle was that their army had behaved with impeccable bravery, never breaking ranks at the end and going down to defeat with great courage.

CHAPTER EIGHT

A SECOND FLODDEN
(Solway Moss, 1542)

It was the battle which broke a King's heart and led to his humiliation and death.

The King was James V of Scotland and the battle was at Solway Moss. It closely resembled Flodden both in its Border locale and in its devastating effect on Scottish morale.

James took vigorous action against his own recalcitrant peoples, most notably the Highlanders and Border reivers.

The King re-organised his armed forces and became so confident that in November, 1542, he marched out of Edinburgh with 20,000 men, keen to invade England. He had been stung into action through English incursions which had resulted in Roxburgh, Kelso and twenty villages being burned.

Part of the army under the King went to Lochmaben while 10,000 men commanded by Oliver Sinclair advanced to Langholm and then into England.

The King remained at his headquarters far from the scene of action which was a strategic mistake because his forces were riven with dissension and there was no clear leadership at the front. This was to prove fatal in the ensuing clash.

These disagreements had religious origins. Henry the Eighth had renounced the authority of the Pope in order to divorce his wives and there were many in Scotland who inclined to follow his example but the Reformation north of the border was largely the outcome of a rational criticism into which all classes of society entered and even some of the clergy welcomed change because the Church had become too worldly and full of ignorance and vice. But James did not imitate his uncle Henry. He had shown more severity than tact in suppressing his fierce, arrogant and ambitious nobles and needed the powerful help of the Church. Besides a natural pride prevented him from acting as a mere second to Henry.

However, the English King continued to pressurise James to side with him in his campaign against the papacy. He tried to bribe nobles and was constantly trying to undermine James.

Thus the Scottish forces hardly presented a united front to the enemy.

A SECOND FLODDEN

Many of the nobles in Sinclair's army resented being commanded by the King's favourite and the Protestants among them were suspicious about being placed where casualties would be heaviest.

Their orders were to cross the Esk and harry the country as far as they could penetrate.

The Scots deteriorated into a disorganised rabble when a force of three thousand English soldiers and cavalry under Lord Wharton appeared on the horizon at Solway Moss between the Water of Leven and the Esk.

The English were superior in the cavalry arm and were highly disciplined and well organised while the Scots continued to argue about who the leader was as the battle commenced.

It was all over quickly and ended in humiliation for the Scots.

The English wisely struck fast and hard while the Scots were trying to form their ranks and the result was total confusion.

Although outnumbered, the English attacked with drive, energy and flair and their cavalry in particular performed with great courage and decisiveness.

The Scottish forces, already disorganised, turned and fled and the battle was transformed into a rout.

Twelve hundred Scots were taken prisoner, including earls, barons and lairds, as well as standards and much equipment.

But the defeat had reverberations greater than the military one.

James's humiliation was seen as Fate's condemnation of his reign. This was exacerbated by the fact that James had always been ruthless and arrogant in his treatment of his nobles.

He did share one thing in common with Henry the Eighth - a manic, passionate nature which could either be euphoric or plunge into black, savage depression.

Following Solway Moss his fuming and raging became almost incoherent and he died the following month at Falkland Palace.

He was aged 30 and his untimely death meant that his heir and only lawful child was a one-week-old baby girl, Mary Stuart, who later was the ill fated Mary, Queen of Scots.

The baby meant a regency government in Scotland which was a godsend to Henry the Eighth and meant the English could easily influence events north of the border. Also, the nobles captured at Solway Moss could be turned into effective English agents.

It was a further encroachment of the more powerful southern neighbour into Scotland whose confidence had been gradually eroded over the years since Bannockburn.

CHAPTER NINE

A QUEEN'S LAST STAND
(Langside, 1568)

The figure of Mary, Queen of Scots has been shrouded in so much myth and romanticism over the years that it is difficult to discriminate between fact and fiction.

Mary Stewart was beautiful, manipulative, sophisticated, passionate, naive, unlucky and reckless.

Her upbringing had been totally unsuitable for the future Queen of Scotland. She was reared in the Catholic court of France where the divine right of royalty was taken for granted and the authoritarian rule of the monarch was viewed as the only defence against barbarism.

She returned to her own country where despotism was despised and where a fervent Protestantism was in the ascendancy.

The one thing her subjects could not tolerate with regards to her policies was her determination to restore priests to positions of power.

Her court and much of her realm rose against her and Mary was imprisoned in Lochleven Castle in June, 1567, where she signed a deed of abdication. Six weeks later her son was crowned in Stirling and her half-brother, the Earl of Moray, was appointed regent.

A gifted man, Moray would have made an exceptional monarch. His arch enemy was the Earl of Arran who had plotted deviously to further his claims to the throne and now felt his best chances lay with Mary.

On the night of 2nd May, 1568, thanks to Arran's plotting, Mary escaped from her imprisonment and an escort carried her to Cadzow Castle where her sympathisers rallied.

Nine earls, nine bishops, eighteen lords and a hundred barons with their numerous followers gathered under her banner.

Moray was in Glasgow when he heard what had happened and he at once mustered together a force of around four thousand men which gathered at what is present day Bridgeton.

Mary's forces numbered six thousand but they were a mixed bunch compared to Moray's seasoned, disciplined troops.

On the 13th of May, Moray's scouts told him Mary's army was moving from Hamilton in a westerly direction along the south bank of the Clyde. She wanted to reach Dumbarton Castle, held for her by Lord Fleming, and with this end in view she marched her men to Rutherglen and then proposed to make a wide detour to avoid Glasgow and Moray's army. Her planned route was through Langside, Crookston and Paisley towards the River Clyde which she planned to cross at a ford a little above Dumbarton.

Moray astutely guessed what his opponents were up to and spies confirmed his suspicions. He determined that Mary should never reach Dumbarton Rock which was an impregnable fortress.

Deciding to stop her at Langside, then a village a few miles south of Glasgow which stood on a small hill across which ran Mary's route, Moray's cavalry quickly blocked Mary's way and they were closely followed by the infantry.

Moray's army had time to deploy in an orderly fashion before Mary's forces arrived on the scene and they did so effectively, the right wing being in the village, then the cavalry and the left which extended to the summit of what is now Queen's Park, the centre being held by the guns.

From Rutherglen, Mary's forces marched to Mount Florida where they discovered for the first time that their route was blocked.

The two armies now confronted each other across a cleft in the land.

The Queen's general was the Earl of Argyll who had no great martial gifts and was heartily disliked by just about everybody. His only battle plan was to use his superior numbers and simply win by brute force.

Mary wanted to be in the forefront of her troops to encourage them but she was persuaded to move back out of the danger zone. With a small escort, she galloped to Cathcart Castle and stood on a mound viewing the battle site.

Hostilities began with a cannonade on either side but the balls of iron and stone fell harmlessly into a valley, although the din was deafening.

The Queen's vanguard advanced since it was obvious that Moray's battle plan was to stay on the defensive and block the path of Mary's army and her troops would have to force their way through to reach the Clyde.

Commanded by Lord Claud Hamilton, the Queen's vanguard moved down the slope of the hill and tried to force the passage of a lane leading to Langside.

When Hamilton's men had become packed into the lane, some of

Moray's infantry who had lain hidden behind hedges opened fire at point blank range, pouring fussilades into the packed ranks which fell back into the valley again. There they rallied and tried once more to force their way into the lane.

Moray's left wing was charged by the Queen's cavalry but stood its ground and, being resolute pikemen, drove back the horsemen.

The main fighting took place close to the village in a sunken road and amongst gardens where the soldiers on both sides were crammed tightly together and found it virtually impossible to manoeuvre or deploy. The struggle was fierce and hand-to-hand but it was difficult to bring the weighty pikes into play.

Moray's army was on higher ground and were better disciplined. They also had greater confidence in their commanders and gradually won the upper hand, pushing Mary's men downhill.

Moray despatched the Macfarlanes, a ferocious Highland clan, to deliver a fatal blow to Mary's forces and they charged down on their enemies, yelling their fierce war cries and wielding their bloodstained claymores.

Mary's men broke and ran and the battle turned into a rout.

But Moray had given strict orders that there should be no more bloodshed than necessary and once the battle was won he was able to restrain his disciplined army from wholesale slaughter. It would, after all, have been a case of Scots killing Scots and there were enough outsiders willing to do that.

The battle, although decisive, had only lasted three quarters of an hour. Mary had lost more than 300 dead and many more injured or captured while Moray's casualties were relatively few.

The battle had three immediate consequences - it meant Protestantism became the dominant religion, the auld alliance with France was broken and Mary Stewart's dynastic ambitions were shattered forever.

Queen Mary soon realised that all was lost and fled southwards, seeking sanctuary with her jealous cousin Elizabeth. This eventually led to long years of imprisonment, culminating in Mary's eventual execution.

CHAPTER TEN

THE GREAT WARLORD
(Philiphaugh, 1645)

Like Mary, James Graham, the Marquis of Montrose, is a figure shrouded in mystery and romance and his character has been clouded by writers and poets since his dramatic execution.

He was in reality highly complex and was neither the clear-cut hero or villain which opposing sides maintained.

He was undoubtedly a charismatic figure who was able to lead and inspire tough clansmen on wild adventures and who retained their loyalty to the end.

He was also a visionary, a poet and a mystic with a suicidal devotion to his own beliefs and he incorporated his philosophy in a few pithy lines:-

'He either fears his Fate too much,
Or his deserts are small,
That puts it not unto the Touch,
To win or lose it all.'

He also earned his place in the annals of military history. In one glorious year of vigorous campaigning his ragtag army won stunning victories over vastly superior forces, in the process marching over huge tracts of countryside to perform his elaborate tactics.

His political affiliations varied wildly throughout his colourful career.

When the General Assembly met in St. Mungo's Cathedral in 1638 to depose the Scottish bishops, Montrose, as an elder of the church, was one of its members and he denounced King Charles 1st in his arrogant over-stepping of the royal prerogative by forcing a Book of Common Prayer upon and generally anglicising the northern Presbyterians. Up to this point Montrose, aged 26, had been an average aristocrat of his time - educated at St. Andrews University where he loved sport and gambling before going on a grand European tour. He signed the National Covenant (an anti-Royalist petition defending the Church of Scotland, enforcing its independence and attacking the Papacy) and organised the rebel army, leading troops against the Earl of Huntly and beating royalist forces at the Battle o' the Brig o' Dee.

But Montrose was gradually becoming disillusioned with the civil turmoil engendered by the Covenant. While negotiating with Charles, to whom he still retained an emotional loyalty, he was busy putting forward solutions in Covenanting councils but gradually his royalist sympathies came to the fore, especially when it was revealed that his arch enemy and champion of the Kirk, Archibald Campbell, Earl of Argyll, was being touted as a future dictator.

Montrose accused Campbell of treason and upset his former Covenanting colleagues. He refused to support the Scottish Parliament's union with the English Roundheads, effectively set up by the Solemn League and Covenant of 1643, and was imprisoned for five months in Edinburgh Castle.

Although still courted to take command of the Covenanting forces, he had made his mind up and turned down such blandishments. From now on he was to be a King's man or nothing.

At the age of 32 he joined Charles at Oxford and convinced him of his loyalty, receiving a commission as lieutenant general in Scotland and embarking on the most exciting period of his life.

In August, 1644, he was in the Highlands, raising his army from among a wild rabble who recognised the opportunity of striking a blow against the Campbells.

His forces were also boosted by an Ulster contingent led by the fierce warrior Alasdair MacColla, a MacDonald with a bitter hatred of the Clan Campbell and who had great strength and military expertise. He commanded two thousand men, composed of Catholic veterans of Irish wars and Highland refugees. Their specialty was the notorious Highland Charge which involved firing a single volley from their muskets then charging the enemy with wooden shields and broadswords, a ferocious, screaming mass of clansmen with their blood up and a decisive tactic which usually led to the Covenanters taking to their heels, many of them being cut down as they fled the onslaught.

Capturing Perth after a ferocious clash beneath its walls when the Royalist force decimated an army three times its size, Montrose determined to win Scotland for Charles and also divert enemy troops from England. He marched to Aberdeen which was quickly taken but the bold Marquis for once had a moral lapse, allowing his troops to ransack the city in an orgy of rape and pillage (more than a hundred peaceful citizens were brutally murdered) which caused great bitterness in the north east against his forces.

The Royalist army then headed through Strathbogie to Speyside and turned south through Badenoch to Atholl before wheeling east through Angus to approach Aberdeen once more.

Argyll was now in pursuit and the Royalists destroyed anything that might sustain their enemies while the Covenanters cruelly punished anyone remotely suspected of helping the rebels.

Winter bogged down the pursuit and Alasdair suggested a daring march through the mountains to fall on the Argyll heartlands. This was carried out, bringing carnage to Inveraray at Christmas and Argyll, racing to rescue his homelands, ended up fleeing down Loch Fyne in a galley, leaving his clansmen to their fate.

The jubilant Royalists then withdrew to the north, crossing into Lochaber and marching up the Great Glen where they were caught in a pincer movement between the Earl of Seaforth marching down from Inverness and fresh troops rallied by Argyll coming up from Inverlochy.

But Montrose and Alasdair were not so easily put down and they turned into the hills at the south end of Loch Ness where they doubled back behind the snowy mountains and caught Argyll's army by surprise in the rear. More than 1500 Campbell clansmen were slaughtered and the bards of Keppoch celebrated the event for decades afterwards.

Montrose and his army went on to a succession of stunning victories at Auldearn, Alford and Kilsyth.

In a brilliant year he had cleared much of Scotland of the King's enemies and if the Royalist forces south of the border had been even remotely as competent and ruthless then Charles would not have lost his head and the course of British history would have been changed.

But already national events were working against Montrose. He was unable to recruit the support of the nobility and had antagonised various factions. Meanwhile, Alasdair left his side to continue his own personal vendetta against the Campbells of Argyll and a lack of an intelligence arm to Montrose's forces meant that he consistently underestimated his opponents and was in the dark with regards to their actions. At Philiphaugh outside Selkirk this was to prove calamitous on 13th September, 1645.

Here Montrose finally came up against a worthy opponent - David Leslie, the best of the Covenanting generals, brilliant and brutal, who was marching north to deal with the upstart at the head of a force of six thousand men more than five thousand of which were cavalry.

The Royalists moved up the Tweed in the vain hope of raising the Border clans and camped on a strong position in front of a hill, the other three sides being protected by the Ettrick and the Yarrow rivers.

At daybreak a dense autumn mist lay over the camp and the sentries could not see the approach of Leslie's horsemen who had forded the Ettrick during the night, although pickets had vaguely warned of an enemy force in the area.

As the sun broke through the greyness the Covenant troopers were ready to charge while the Royalists were still finishing their breakfast.

Montrose was billeted in a lodging at Selkirk when the alarm was raised. He jumped on a horse and galloped to his camp where he found his men fighting for their lives while some of their colleagues had quickly deserted at the first charge.

Fortunately for the Royalists they had taken the precaution of building up defensive earthworks and these proved vital in fending off attack after attack which the Covenanters, sensing victory, rained down on them.

Gradually the rebels were beaten back behind dry-stone dykes beside a farm and fought hand-to-hand until more than four hundred were cut down.

Montrose rallied a hundred horsemen and led them in a mad charge which was repeated again and again but each time the Royalists were decimated by superior forces.

The remainder of Leslie's cavalry, on the opposite bank of the Ettrick, saw the brave but futile efforts of the Royalists, forded the river and attacked from the flank.

Six hundred Royalists had stood bravely and defiantly against a vastly superior enemy force. Only a handful survived, among them Montrose who miraculously was unhurt and was prepared to die in action. But he was talked out of this by his immediate entourage, their argument being that his King would need his services in future. He rode to Clydesdale then northwards and soon was taking refuge in the Perthshire hills.

He left behind prisoners who were executed as were their camp followers, six hundred people altogether. His lieutenants, who had surrendered in the belief that their lives would be spared, were either beheaded or hung.

Montrose tried vainly to raise another army before fleeing abroad where he was feted as a hero.

When told of his King's execution, Montrose locked himself in his room for two days, devastated with grief. Then he determined to write Charles's epitaph "in blood and wounds" and set about recruiting a force of mercenaries which invaded the north of Scotland from Sweden via the Orkneys on behalf of Charles 11.

But he had lost that precious luck which Napoleon once said all successful generals must have. He blundered into a rudimentary trap at Carbisdale where his small troop was decimated by a charge of dragoons from woodlands.

Montrose had his horse shot under him but he escaped on foot to the glens where one night he sought shelter from the laird of Assynt.

This was one of the few instances of a fugitive being betrayed for gold. There was, of course, a price on Montrose's head and Assynt betrayed his guest to Government troops.

Montrose was taken to Edinburgh on a cart, bound and barehead, and preceded by the hangman as he was taken up the Royal Mile.

As he passed Moray House his eyes met those of Argyll looking out from behind a half closed blind.

Having been tried in his absence and convicted, he knew what to expect and composed his farewell to the world as he lay in prison:

'Let them bestow on ev'ry airt a limb;
Open all my veins, that I may swim
To Thee my Saviour, in that crimson lake;
Then place my pur-boil'd head upon a stake;
Scatter my ashes, throw them in the air;
Lord (since Thou know'st where all these atoms are)
I'm hopeful, once Thou'lt recollect my dust,'
And confident Thou'lt raise me with the just.'

Dressed immaculately in scarlet and silver lace with white gloves, silk stockings and ribboned shoes - as one eye witness put it, more like a bridegroom than a convicted criminal - Montrose was hanged then disembowelled at the Mercat Cross.

In 1888 his remains were entombed in a splendid marble memorial in St. Giles. By then the legend had well and truly taken over from harsh reality.

CHAPTER ELEVEN

MIRACLE AND MASSACRE
(Dunbar, 1650)

The people of Scotland were so horrified at the execution - or judicial murder as they saw it - of King Charles 1st that they promptly declared his son Charles the rightful ruler.

The young king disembarked at the mouth of the Spey on 23rd of June, 1650, and signed both the National Covenant and the Solemn League, two documents assuring a measure of religious independence to his Scottish subjects and loyal supporters.

He was installed at Falkland Palace and was lectured to by relays of Presbyterian ministers keen to enforce their dogmas on him.

All of this naturally made the English Parliamentarians, who thought they had got rid of the Stewarts once and for all, extremely angry. Oliver Cromwell in particular was not amused and called on the Scots for *"all God's elect to unite with their fellow elect in England"*.

This appeal fell on deaf ears and Cromwell, who always believed he was obeying the orders of the Almighty, felt the urge to subjugate Scotland and duly crossed the Border with an invasion force of 16,000 highly trained Roundheads, a fleet following up the East coast in support.

Cromwell's first object was the subjugation of Edinburgh from where he intended to rule the country.

David Leslie, the commander who had finally quashed the flame of Montrose, astutely foresaw what was afoot and positioned his army to block the invasion force and despite repeated attempts to break through to Leith and then Queensferry so that he could link up with his supplies offshore, Cromwell was forced to withdraw his troops to Dunbar.

The Scottish army had marched out initially more than 26,000 strong but it had gradually been weakened by purges enforced by the Kirk ministers who wanted to get rid of the more ungodly elements. In the process they also managed to get rid of the more professional, hardened soldiers (around 4,000), leaving behind a motley assembly of *"minister's sons, clerks and such other sanctified creatures who hardly ever saw or heard of any sword but that of the Spirit"*. It was also controlled by a parliamentary committee, modelled on a Kirk session, made up largely of religious folk who saw fit to over-rule

Leslie when they thought his shrewd judgement misguided. They were more interested in the Bible than military manuals.

Realising it was the ministers of the Kirk who had the real power, Cromwell addressed his passionate pleas for peace and reconciliation to them, ending with the famous words, *"I beseech you, in the bowels of Christ, think it possible you may be mistaken!"*

But again his pleas fell on deaf ears and he realised the Scots could only be ruled by force.

But the Ironsides, as Cromwell's troops were known, were in dire straits as the summer progressed.

Leslie had carried out a scorched earth policy in Berwickshire and East Lothian and also launched vicious raids against the enemy. In addition, disease had ravaged the ranks of the Ironsides and on top of famine this meant that Cromwell could only call on around 11,000 reasonably fit men. The Scottish force against him was double this and now occupied commanding heights on Doon Hill outside Dunbar above the English forces. A second Scottish force barred the exit to the south.

Cromwell was trapped. To fight his way out would prove a costly exercise against superior forces and adverse ground conditions. To retreat by sea was impossible because the weather was stormy and, anway, there was not enough ships to carry all the men. In addition, while embarkation took place the Ironsides would be more or less at the mercy of the Scots.

But Cromwell was nothing if not confident that God was on his side. Perhaps he was right, judging by the way events unfolded. Certainly on the eve of the decisive battle he told his troops, *"We have much hope in the Lord of Whose mercy we have had large experience."*

And Cromwell's hoped-for miracle took place.

That same evening the English could not believe their eyes. The Scots were filing down in columns from their vantage point onto the plain.

The reason for this was that the ministers had once more taken charge of tactics and had over-ruled Leslie's better judgement. He had forcibly argued that all the Scots needed to do was sit tight and starve Cromwell into surrender. But the preachers, too, were convinced God was on their side and they could not lose so they led their flock down to the enemy. They fully expected the English to flee.

Cromwell, who just hours previously had grimly told his

immediate entourage, "We are upon an engagement very difficult!" now declared, "The Lord hath delivered them into my hands!"

The Scottish forces had a deep burn on their left and behind them was a steep hill. Unless they achieved immediate success they would find it difficult to deploy.

Before dawn, the English moved into position, crossing the burn, chasing off pickets and facing up to their enemy in a line, successfully hemming in the Scots.

Cromwell on horseback rallied his troops, prayed, exhorted them to do their best then charged at dawn.

The Scots were totally unprepared for this aggressive action.

The English soldiers were tougher, more experienced and better disciplined. Severe fighting took place and there were heavy casualties on both sides but gradually the Ironsides fought their way through the front ranks containing the cream of Leslie's army. The Scots veterans were quickly decimated by succeeding waves of Roundheads and the gentlemen behind them who should have come to their support promptly turned and fled the field in a blind panic.

Two Scottish regiments vainly tried to hold the line and fought to the death while their comrades were cut down as they ran off, casting away their weapons.

The final dreadful tally for the Scots who had started in such a strong position was four thousand dead and ten thousand prisoners.

It was the end of the Kirk party and the meddling of preachers in military affairs.

It also meant Cromwell was master of Scotland and he duly kept the country under a systematic rule and military occupation for the next eight years.

The Royalist nobility tried to restore Charles to his English throne with the remnants of Scottish troops but they were decisively defeated by Cromwell at Worcester and the King again fled abroad as did many Scottish supporters while others were imprisoned or reduced to poverty.

CHAPTER TWELVE

THE PITCHFORK ARMY
(Drumclog and Bothwell Bridge, 1679)

Like Montrose, John Graham of Claverhouse, 1st Viscount Dundee, is a character who was both adored and reviled.

He was a bloodthirsty and cruel oppressor to the Covenanters and a hero to the Jacobites, thus earning himself two nicknames - 'Bloody Clavers' and 'Bonnie Dundee'.

Born in 1649, he was descended from the Grahams of Kincardine and studied at St. Andrews University where he specialised in "the arts of war" before entering foreign service.

On his return home he was appointed a troop captain in the King's Own Regiment where he was promoted to colonel.

The country was riven with religious dissent and field sermons were spreading with fanatics haranguing their flocks about the iniquities of the King. Frequently these gatherings had armed elements and scouts were posted to look out for troops of horse whose patrols were scouring the countryside, putting down any sign of rebellion.

Claverhouse rejected the claims of the Covenanting extremists who he believed were dangerous anarchists and supported Charles 11 and the rule of the Establishment.

But Claverhouse seriously underestimated the military support behind the Covenanters. Moderates might not agree with the violent rhetoric of the preachers but they had some keen military minds in their ranks as the King's troops were to find out.

General unrest was brought to a head by a murder on Magus Moor.

James Sharp was a detested presbyterian prelate who had earned the hatred of every faithful Covenanter in Scotland.

On the 3rd of May, 1679, while driving across Magus Moor, his coach was stopped by a party of his enemies and on his knees, praying for his life, he was slashed to death by swords.

The two main assassins then fled to the shelter of the Covenanters in Clydesdale who were in the mood for insurrection.

On the anniversary of the King's restoration they made a bonfire of the Royal Acts of Parliament at Rutherglen Cross near Glasgow, a scene which attracted all the malcontents of the area who quickly decamped to nearby Strathaven as Claverhouse was despatched to deal with them.

He came across them drawn up in order of battle at Drumclog near Loudon Hill on the morning of Sunday, the 1st of June.

The Covenanters were well positioned with a deep ditch in front of them and boglands on their flanks. They had four battalions of foot and three squadrons of horse, perhaps a thousand men all told.

The two forces commenced firing at each other but their musketry proved ineffectual.

Claverhouse was keen to come to grips with the enemy but could not find a suitable path which would get him close.

But while he was debating what to do, the Covenanters, led by William Cleland, charged down on them, throwing the King's dragoons into disorder, killing thirty six of them.

Claverhouse's horse had its belly ripped open by a pitchfork as he fled the field.

A Royalist prisoner was shot out of hand and the rest released while the body of a relative of Claverhouse was horribly mutilated by the Covenanters in the mistaken belief that it was the hated Royalist commander.

The dragoons retreated to Glasgow where Claverhouse put up barricades in the belief that the city would be overwhelmed.

The Covenanters did mount an attack but it was a half hearted affair and they were easily beaten off.

However, the victory at Drumclog had boosted the morale of the rebels who came pouring into the west of Scotland, arming themselves with whatever weapons they could lay their hands on - muskets, pikes, swords, pitchforks and scythes.

The Covenanting army now stood at around six thousand and the ranks were swelling by the day.

In response, the Government mustered an army of fifteen thousand and the two forces faced each other at the bridge over the Clyde at Bothwell.

The Covenanters trusted in the Lord delivering their enemies into their hands and made no attempt at military organisation.

They held their end of the bridge for as long as possible, pouring fussilades into the Royalist troops but when their ammunition became exhausted the rag-tag army was forced to fall back.

The Royalist troops marched across the bridge and surrounded their disorganised enemies.

More than twelve hundred Covenanters were taken prisoner and tried in Edinburgh, many being deported. Two were executed and five others hanged on Magus Moor.

Claverhouse proceeded to mount a terror campaign, torching the farms of anyone suspected of having covenanting sympathies.

CHAPTER THIRTEEN

THE VICTORY AND THE MARTYR
(Killiecrankie, 1689)

In November, 1688, William of Orange disembarked at Torbay and the 'Glorious Revolution' that was to put him on the throne began.

James V11, the last Stewart King, fled to France and Claverhouse burst into tears at the news.

The sympathies of the country were split in two, some for William, some for James.

A special Convention of the nobility and clergy met in Edinburgh in March, 1689, to decide who to support, eventually coming down in favour of William.

But, foreseeing the verdict, Claverhouse quit the capital and raised troops in the north for the Jacobite cause where the wild Highlanders called him 'Dark John of the Battles'.

The famous song *'Bonnie Dundee'* - with its stirring chorus *'For it's up wi' the bonnets o' Bonnie Dundee'* - depicts the departure of Claverhouse from the capital.

A chronicler described him as *"the haughty cavalier on his sorrel-coloured charger, his wealth of rich dark curls setting off his beautiful features as he headed his troops on his famous march out of Edinburgh."*

He was promptly declared a traitor and, after raising King James's standard on Dundee Law, retreated with a small force into the Highlands to gather recruits.

Hot on his trail was General Hugh Mackay of Scourie with his Williamite army.

Claverhouse had to be the arch diplomat as he tried to keep his disorganised army of more than four thousand together. There was the danger of internecine clan feuding breaking out and his soldiers were not above going off to raid rivals when they were supposed to be on the march.

Military matters came to a head in midsummer and they centred on Blair Castle which commanded the passes into the Dee and the Spey.

Both sides knew how vital it was to hold this formidable keep.

It belonged to the Marquis of Atholl whose son occupied it in the name of William.

On July 26th, Claverhouse's forces arrived at the castle while Mackay's men, also around four thousand strong, gathered at Dunkeld.

Claverhouse held a council of war at which the strategic options were debated.

All of his army were not yet assembled which meant they were currently outnumbered by three to two. Some clan chiefs wanted to retire until they were up to strength but others urged that they fight, stressing the high morale of the men. Claverhouse was of this latter opinion.

It was decided to give battle but Sir Ewen Cameron of Lochiel (reputed to have killed an English officer by biting out his throat - "the sweetest bite" according to Sir Ewen) asked their leader not to expose himself to possible injury during the fray.

Claverhouse argued that his men would think him cowardly if he led from the rear and declared he would devote one "shear-darg" (or day's harvesting) to the King's cause but would never again hazard his life during the campaign. It was to prove a fateful if courageous decision.

The chiefs grudgingly accepted their commander's view. They had little choice with a man of Claverhouse's fiery, domineering personality.

Early on the morning of the 27th of July, Mackay marched out of Dunkeld and by ten o'clock had reached the southern end of the Pass of Killiecrankie.

This was a narrow gorge with the River Garry flowing swiftly through its middle and high, wooded, mountain slopes on either side.

It would have been easy to ambush Mackay's troops in such a defile but Claverhouse was more interested in a full-scale pitched battle and he allowed his enemies to make their way slowly and cautiously down through the Pass all day.

After more open ground was reached, Mackay's men deployed for battle, facing towards Blair and relieved to be out of the confines of the Pass.

Some Highlanders were seen coming down the glen and Mackay deployed to face them, only to discover they were a diversionary party and that the main enemy army was in fact gathering on a hilltop on the right flank. Mackay had to hastily re-arrange his positions which were now shown to be in a decidedly unfavourable spot with the river behind them and a steep hill before them.

As the long, sunny afternoon waned, both armies faced each other. Mackay refused to move uphill and Claverhouse refused to charge when the sun was in the eyes of his men.

It was eight o'clock when the Highlanders finally advanced, casting aside their plaids and charging down in their shifts, screaming and yelling their war cries, wielding their claymores and crashing into the enemy ranks in a devastating, frenzied wave after discharging their muskets and flinging them away at almost point blank range.

According to one eye witness, *"nothing was heard for some few moments but the sullen and hollow clashes of the broadswords, with the dismal groans and cries of dying and wounded men."*

Claverhouse, on horseback, led his mounted troops against enemy cavalry who turned and galloped off in fear of their lives.

Mackay's soldiers were gradually overwhelmed and only one regiment managed to get across the river in an orderly retreat.

The Government forces lost two thousand men in dead, wounded and prisoners. The Highlanders had nine hundred killed.

But although it was a technical victory for the rebels, Lochiel's worst fears were realised and Claverhouse was killed.

He was riding forward urging his men on when a musket bullet struck him in the side and knocked him out of his saddle.

His officers raced to his side but he was dying.

"How goes the day?" he asked.

"Well for King James," came the reply.

"If it is well for him, it matters less for me," and as he closed his eyes Claverhouse could hear the victorious cheers of his Highlanders. It was an end he would have wished.

Wrapped in two tartan plaids, he was buried that night at a mournful ceremony in the little church of Blair.

With their inspiring commander gone at the moment of victory, the dispirited clansmen were unable to follow up their advantage.

Leaderless and fraught with dissension, in August they retreated from Dunkeld and, after some sporadic fighting during the winter, were eventually defeated the following spring at the Haughs of Cromdale.

But although he died a martyr, Claverhouse had carried the fiery cross of the Jacobite cause forward, taking over from Montrose when it came to legendary, inspiring leadership. He had shown what could be done with a properly organised Highland army and his venture in 1689 was to be a model for the Risings of 1715 and 1745.

CHAPTER FOURTEEN

THE RUNNING BATTLE
(Sherrifmuir, 1715)

If ever a Royal family was jinxed with bad luck, it was the House of Stewart and this was most dramatically illustrated during the Rebellions in support of them in 1715 and 1745.

Much of the support of the Stewart cause was motivated more by a desire to tear up the 1707 Treaty of Union and dissolve Scotland's amalgamation with England. This feeling was strongest in the Highlands where the Gaelic culture correctly felt itself under threat.

After eight years most of the articles of the Union had been breached by the English politicians who paid no heed to the needs of people north of the border. Scottish law, religion and industry were ignored and the rights of the English took constant precedence.

The Scots were crying out for a leader of the calibre of Bruce, Montrose or Claverhouse to lead them out of this predicament. But regrettably no great leader was forthcoming. However, the general feeling was that at least a Stewart King on the throne would have some Scottish sympathies, currently sadly lacking among the British nobility.

The majority of the clans were now in the fighting mood to take to the field to bring back the Stewarts who they viewed as their only saviours.

Things came to a head in August, 1715, when the Earl of Mar, disgusted with the way Scotland was viewed from London, sailed from the Thames, determined to raise his country for 'the King across the water'.

All the leading Jacobites were invited to a great hunting expedition on Mar's estate which was a plausible subterfuge for calling a huge council of war.

They declared themselves for King James V111 and raised his standard.

The Government, sensing what was afoot, passed an Act outlawing any noble who supported the Jacobite cause but this had no effect on the rebels who rallied at Braemar and declared James the rightful King of Britain.

The Fiery Cross was despatched through the glens to raise the clansmen and they responded enthusiastically.

Five hundred Mackintoshes started the campaign by capturing Inverness.

By mid-September Mar's army was at Dunkeld where it was reinforced by four thousand men from Atholl and Breadalbane and a few days later Perth was taken while Jacobite citizens took over Aberdeen, Brechin and Dundee.

The Duke of Argyll was put in charge of the Hanoverian army in Scotland. It comprised two thousand regulars boosted by the same number in volunteers raised in Lowland towns.

But Mar's force by this time was more than 12,000 strong and the Government knew it had a real fight on its hands.

Argyll was at Stirling while Mar remained at Perth.

But the Jacobites were forced into action by news that a force of foreign mercenaries was marching north to help Argyll.

Mar intended crossing the Forth by a ford near Aberfoyle but Argyll's spies reported back that the Jacobites were on the march and the Hanoverians broke camp to intercept the rebels at Sheriffmuir, two miles east of Dunblane.

Because he had despatched a force southwards in a futile encircling action and because some clansmen had deserted, Mar's force had been reduced to 8,000 while Argyll's had been swollen to 3,500 thanks to troop reinforcements from garrisons at Glasgow and Edinburgh.

The rebels were obviously still vastly superior in number and should have won the day.

But Argyll was a shrewd professional soldier whereas Mar was an amateur with delusions of grandeur.

He did have the gift of the gab and before the battle he made *"a very fine speech"* to his troops which one of his commanders regarded sourly as *"the only good action of his life"*. Because of his political vacillations he had earned the soubriquet 'Bobbing John'. This indecision was to prove fatal to the Jacobite cause.

So instead of charging the enemy with his superior numbers, 'Bobbing John' decided to hold yet another council of war.

The clan chiefs angrily declared that the only tactic must be to fight their hated enemy Argyll otherwise the Highlanders would desert in droves.

The two armies then set off towards each other on either side of a gentle hill and as soon as they came within sight of the enemy the Jacobites fired their muskets, flung them away with their plaids, tied their shirts under their crotches then charged, yelling madly, and swinging their claymores.

Argyll's right wing was overwhelmed and dispersed in disarray towards Dunblane.

But it was a different tale elsewhere on the battlefield.

On Mar's left the Highland charge had been contained by the steadiness of ranks of dragoons. The clansmen were driven back and, before they could reorganise, Argyll's cavalry thundered into them, putting them into rout, the Hanoverian infantry eagerly taking up the pursuit.

The battlefield now presented a bizarre spectacle. The right wing of each army had been victorious over their immediate enemy positions and were hot in pursuit, leaving the actual site of the hostilities empty save for the dead and wounded. To the north Argyll's cavalry was chasing Mar's Highlanders; to the south the Jacobites were cutting down the fleeing Hanoverian troops.

Each right wing was flushed with victory while each left wing was in dissarray.

This led to the famous song -

'There's some say that we wan,
And some say that they wan,
And some say that nane wan at a', man;
But ae thing I'm sure,
That at Sherra-muir
A battle there was, that I saw, man;
And we ran, and they ran,
And they ran, and we ran
And we ran, and they ran awa, man.'

Mar retreated to Perth and when Argyll returned to the field he found Highlanders occupying a hill but both sides were exhausted and the Hanoverians allowed their enemies to draw off.

The Hanoverians had lost six hundred and Mar eight hundred men.

Technically the battle was a draw but in the long term it proved to be a Hanoverian victory because it bought time while Government reinforcements poured into Scotland, finally subduing the rebellion.

With typically bad timing, King James landed in Scotland once it was all over and promptly retreated abroad again, taking Mar with him.

CHAPTER FIFTEEN

EARLY ONE MORNING
(Prestonpans, 1745)

When Charles Edward Stuart, the Young Pretender, son of James Vlll and the man known to history as 'Bonnie Prince Charlie,' landed on Eriskay in July, 1745, it was a reckless gamble which no-one initially believed had any chance of success.

But Charles was a charismatic personality with a driving passion to win back the throne for the Stewart cause and he was able to win over clan chiefs who came to see him. These were tough, experienced warriors and it is a measure of the power of Charles' eloquence that he was able to persuade them to risk all for his cause.

Lochiel declared after a lengthy talk with Charles, *"I will share the fate of my prince and so shall every man over whom nature or fortune has given me any power."*

Within days and starting from nothing, the Prince had Glengarry and Clanranald, Macdonald of Keppoch and Stewart of Ardshiel pledged to his cause.

Charles marched to Glenfinnan where all the clans were ordered to rally. For hours the glen was empty then the disconsolate rebels heard the distant skirl of the pipes and seven hundred Camerons came marching out of the heather-clad hills followed by thousands of others. The Jacobite banner was unfurled and, as cheers split the air and bonnets were flung high, Charles addressed his troops and urged them on to victory.

The Government forces were commanded by Sir John Cope, a capable but unimaginative soldier who seemed indecisive when it came to tackling the rebellion on his doorstep. He had vague notions of marching an army into the Highlands with a view to stopping the rebels and set off for Inverness.

Meanwhile, Charles moved south through Perthshire, gathering recruits en route including Lord George Murray, brother of the Duke of Atholl and a professional soldier who took over the leadership of the Jacobite army.

Cope realised his quarry was eluding him and was threatening Edinburgh so he made for Aberdeen and embarked his army on transports south.

But the Governement forces were too late to stop Charles and his army entering the capital where the Prince held court at Holyrood Palace, parading through the streets in his colourful finery.

Cope landed at Dunbar and hastened to tackle the upstarts.

Charles rallied his troops at Duddingston and they were eager to confront the enemy.

Cope drew his men up on a level plain bordering the Firth of Forth.

Murray led his men onto higher ground so that they were facing the Government troops from a ridge. Cope was forced to re-deploy to face them. Marshland criss-crossed with dykes lay between the two armies and, in addition, there was a deep ditch before the redcoat army and this led to a stalemate. As the sun set, both armies stood where they were and awaited developments.

The Prince held a Council of War when a young volunteer came to Murray, claiming to know a way through the boglands which would lead the Jacobites onto Cope's left flank.

In darkness and silence the rebels moved out towards the campfires of their enemies.

Before dawn, the Highlanders gathered in two disciplined lines close to the slumbering Government troops, having successfully traversed through the marsh, successfully led by their local guide.

An outpost of Cope's troops suddenly spotted them and the alarm was raised but as the mists cleared the Highlanders charged over a field, crouching low, their shields before them, to avoid musket fire.

As at Killiecrankie, the Highland Charge tactics involved pausing at point blank range, firing muskets then charging forward wielding claymores.

The clansmen, shrieking and racing forward, broke the first terrified ranks of the redcoats, many of whom turned and fled towards Edinburgh, being cut down as they retreated.

The battle lasted only minutes, some of the Highlanders in the second line not even taking part in any fighting as Cope's men fled in terror.

By 5 a.m. it was all over.

The final tally was 400 redcoats slain and 700 taken prisoner out of a force of 2,000. The Highlanders had 30 killed and 70 wounded.

Cope galloped off to Coldstream, more than 40 miles away, and ended up in Berwick.

At an official enquiry, Cope was absolved of all blame for the fiasco. Responsibility was placed instead on the *"shameful behaviour"* of his soldiers and he went on to serve his country honourably until he died in 1760.

A famous humourous song was made about the battle called 'Hey Johnnie Cope', the chorus of which is-

'Hey Johnny Cope, are ye waukin' yet?
Or are your drums a beatin' yet?
If ye were waukin' I wad wait,
To gang to the coals i' the mornin'.'

CHAPTER SIXTEEN

VICTORY IN THE RAIN
(Falkirk, 1746)

The Jacobite victory at Prestonpans brought many new recruits flocking to their cause.

Charles had the whole of Scotland under his control apart from the strongholds of Edinburgh and Stirling which still held out.

The rebel army was put at more than five thousand, mostly ferocious fighters from the north, well armed and spoiling for a fight.

The Prince continued to hold court at Edinburgh as the ranks of his followers increased but he was impatient to move south, although his supporters would have been equally content to stay in Scotland and leave England to the Hanoverians.

Charles, with his usual eloquence, won the day over the advice of his immediate entourage and the Jacobite army moved south on November 1st, taking Carlisle and getting as far south as Derby.

It was there that the fateful decision was taken to retreat back north.

Not enough support had appeared for the rebels south of the border and there were fears of being encircled by superior Hanoverian forces.

Charles fiercely argued that the rebels should press on to London where the court was on the point of collapse but for once he was unable to win over his lieutenants.

Arguments have raged ever since over who was right but even after the Jacobites turned back north it did not mean that defeat for them was inevitable, although Charles was never the same man again, having lost his high spirits at Derby and plunging into a defeatist depression uncharacteristic of the opening phases of his campaign.

Cope had been succeeded in the north by General Hawley, an officer who had 8,000 troops under him, including 1300 cavalry.

The Hanoverian forces marched to Falkirk where they were poised to relieve Stirling Castle.

Lord George Murray, fully aware that the morale of his Highlanders had been badly dented after the retreat from Derby, was keen to engage the enemy and marched in their direction.

The armies clashed on Falkirk Muir as the Hanoverian cavalry and the Highlanders raced for the high ground. The Jacobites won and, as torrential rain poured down, three regiments of English dragoons tried to sweep the clansmen off their ridge.

The Jacobites held their fire until the last minute then a fussilade was released at almost point-blank range, throwing the cavalry into disarray.

Just as at Prestonpans, a panic seized the Hanoverian army and they turned and fled.

Some redcoat commanders tried to rally their troops and a brigade of cavalry did manage to break into the Jacobite ranks but their horses were stabbed and the riders killed.

Three regiments on the Hanoverian right did hold their ground and poured a volley into the ranks of the charging Highlanders who, fearing an ambush, drew back to their own lines, thus allowing the Government forces to retire in better order.

Hawley managed to get most of his men through Falkirk and safely on the road to Edinburgh and the Jacobites were unable to pursue due to a lack of cavalry.

Hawley reached Edinburgh where he had erected two gibbets on which he had planned to hang Jacobites. He used them now to string up some of his own cowardly dragoons.

Because of the lack of commitment of the Hanoverian troops, the casualties at Falkirk were not high. The Jacobites lost 32 men killed and 120 wounded while the Hanoverians lost 280 including prisoners.

It was to be the last sweet taste of victory for the Jacobites.

CHAPTER SEVENTEEN

A LAST LAMENT
(Culloden, 1746)

Following their victory at Falkirk, the Jacobites continued their siege of Stirling Castle but there was no sign of the defenders cracking under the strain.

The Hanoverian troops were now put under King George's son, the Duke of Cumberland, a heartless, ruthless brute of a soldier who was, nevertheless, highly competent and determined.

It was now more than five months since Charles had rallied the clans at Glenfinnan and many of the Highlanders grumbled that they now had precious little to show for all their sacrifice and effort.

Many men, weary of being under arms, slipped away to tend to their farming responsibilities and to see their families. The Spring sowing had to be attended to and fields had to be tilled and cattle looked after. The clansmen, irregular troops at the best of times, did not view this as any kind of breach of discipline since they were willing to hasten to their Prince's side should the call go out for them to rally.

Reluctantly, Charles decided to retreat further north into the mountains and decamped for Inverness which was occupied by Government forces under the Earl of Loudon. This garrison soon panicked on being told the Jacobites were approaching and retreated to the Black Isle.

On February 20th, 1746, Charles entered Inverness and by early March both Fort George and Fort Augustus had fallen to them.

Meanwhile, Cumberland was at Aberdeen, laying his plans and gathering his forces. In April he set off westwards and reached Nairn on the 14th.

The Jacobites were encamped at Culloden, seven miles from Inverness near the edge of Drummossie Moor. They decided on a surprise dawn attack, similar to their successful ploy at Prestonpans, but by the time they made their way over bogland in the dark the weary men, straggled over several miles, were well short of their target as dawn approached and the whole project had to be abandoned.

By 7 a.m. the clansmen were back at Culloden and flung themselves exhausted onto the damp heather. Two hours later the alarm was raised - Cumberland's forces were approaching.

In the blustery, rainswept early afternoon, Charles' five thousand tired, demoralised men faced Cumberland's eight thousand heavily armed, professional troops across a mile of moorland.

It was the high noon of the Stuart cause and a test which the charismatic Prince was to fail utterly, sending thousands of his supporters to a grisly doom.

What people forget about the Battle of Culloden (the last fought on British soil) was that up till then the Jacobites were undefeated and were a formidable force in their own Highland strongholds.

Help was on the way from France, the English Jacobites were belatedly rallying and, at the very least, guerrilla tactics (at which the wily Highlanders were expert) could have been used to harass if not defeat the Hanoverian redcoats north of the border.

Everything was in the balance and everything was flung away by the petulant, despairing, fatal decision of Charles Edward Stuart to fight Cumberland's army despite the ground being unsuitable, the Highlanders being exhausted, the Redcoats having superior firepower in artillery and despite the fact that Charles could have mustered a further 3,500 troops out foraging or manning outposts if he had just waited another day.

But Charles' fatal eloquence won the day and the result was disaster for his army.

The Hanoverian guns cut swathes in the standing lines of Highlanders who were awaiting orders.

Angry and frustrated, the clansmen charged forward yelling "Claymore!"

The whole front crashed into the Government ranks and the Redcoats blazed away with musketry and grape-shot at point-blank range.

The Jacobites burst through the first rank and made gashes in the second, yelling and slicing with their broadswords, but they were cut down by the Hanoverian soldiers standing firm, rifles raised, in the third line.

English dragoons marched forward but were repulsed by the Prince's reserves.

However, reinforcements of Hanoverian cavalry soon won the day as the decimated ranks of the Highlanders retreated, their lines being decimated further by cannon and musket balls that buzzed through the pouring rain.

The crisis of the battle had lasted only a few minutes during which a third of the Jacobites had been wiped out.

As the rebels were retreating, Cumberland gave the notorious order that no quarter was to be given. All the wounded on the battlefield were murdered and no prisoners were taken. Fugitives were cut down and slain. The moor was red with blood and as the Hanoverians splashed around on it, performing their grisly task, they looked more like butchers in a slaughterhouse than soldiers.

The whole action had lasted less than an hour but thanks to the foolishness of the Prince his cause was lost forever.

He had wanted to die in battle but had been pulled out of the fighting and for months was a fugitive on the run in the heather before he escaped to France, dying an old, dissipated, disappointed man years later.

His rebellion brought disaster to the Highlands where Government troops brought their own form of ethnic cleansing to the Gaels whose culture and livelihood was largely destroyed.

Roads, forts and garrisons were built to tame the north and any hint of rebellion was quickly extinguished.

The fighting fervour had gone out of the nation, the tartan, the kilt and the bagpipe were banned and it was many years before that martial spirit revived, transformed into the proud Scottish regiments that helped to defeat Napoleon and create the British Empire.